I WILL NEVER GIVE UP
ON GOD AGAIN

From Feeling Abandoned By God To Feeling Embraced By God

By Derek W. Clark

Printed in the United States of America

FIRST EDITION

I WILL NEVER GIVE UP ON GOD AGAIN
WRITTEN BY DEREK W.CLARK
www.NeverGiveUpOnGod.com

Edited by Michael Laemmle
Email: mrlaemmle@gmail.com

Cover design by Adreana Shavers
www.BoldGraphixINC.com

**To Book Derek For Your Upcoming Event
Call 1-800-980-0751**

CONTACT DEREK CLARK AT
Derek@IWillNeverGiveUp.com

www.NeverGiveUpOnGod.com

PUBLISHED BY NEVER LIMIT YOUR LIFE
OFFERING WORKSHOPS AND SEMINARS

www.NeverLimitYourLife.com
ISBN 13: 978-0-615-26735-7

Contents

"We Walk By Faith, Not By Sight"

2 Corinthians 5:7 (King James Version)

1 John 4:9-10 (King James Version)

9 In this was manifested the love of God towards us, because that God sent only begotten Son into the world, that we might live through him.

10 Herein is love, not that we loved God, but that he loved us, and sent his Son to be the propitiation for our sins.

2 Proverbs 3:5-6 (King James Version)

5 Trust in the LORD with all thine heart; and lean not unto thine own understanding.

6 In all thy ways acknowledge him, and he shall direct thy paths.

"I Can Testify That Having Faith in God and Jesus Christ Strengthens Your Spirit. With God's Help, You Too Can Overcome Your Suffering and Be Victorious in Your Life. By Letting Him in Your Heart, You Allow Hope, Faith, Love, Perseverance, Obedience, Endurance, Empathy and Forgiveness To Shape Your Character. What an Awesome Feeling to Know That God Has a Destiny for You. Reach Out and Call to Him. He is The Creator of Life and The Giver of Good".

Dedications

I dedicate this book to my beloved wife, the Joy of my life, and my beautiful, angelic children; Ozmond, Remington, Montgomery and Trayton.

Thank you all for being great examples for me, and for encouraging me to be the best husband, father, and man that I can be. I want you to know that Daddy has been through a lot in his life, and that you will never have to go through what I went through. Also, know that I believe in God with all my heart; that I value and respect His power. He has led me to you, and blessed me with your presence. You're the little angels who have fueled my faith in Him. Despite years of struggle with belief, my love for God has grown. I now firmly believe in His mercy. I know He has forgiven me for my stubbornness, unfaithfulness, and anger. If you ever find yourselves in hard times, pray in humbleness and with pure intent. Do not challenge God, or try to provoke Him; it will only create distance between yourselves and Him. He is your Creator, your Father in Heaven, and is an inexhaustible source of empowering strength to draw from during times of struggle. He is a Heavenly compass, directing you through all of life's rough waters. Have faith! All things are possible through God's miraculous power. There is no need to feel fear in your journey if you walk with God.

TO ALL
THAT ARE SUFFERING

To all the people suffering in this world: TAKE A DEEP BREATH! This current hardship is only one small part of your big, adventurous life. Don't let pain consume your entire existence, and don't use it as an excuse for your downfalls. I know you may feel lost at times, but you have the power to take decisive actions and overcome self-doubt. You will make it if you surround yourself with good friends who make good choices and set good examples. Don't dwell on misfortunes from the past, or blame yourself for circumstances that were beyond your control. Let go of the grief you may have suffered during childhood, and don't let it pollute your mature perspective on life. For too long, I thought I was to blame for my parents abandoning me to foster care. Much later in life, I realized it wasn't my fault. I WAS ONLY FIVE YEARS OLD! I spent many years shouldering a guilt that wasn't rightfully mine.

Don't poison yourself with gloomy emotions or pessimistic outlooks. Don't be a nothing! Be everything you want to be, and never stop dreaming. Your dreams are your own; don't let anyone take them away. Every possibility is within your reach, so long as you have the confidence to take action. Never let anyone convince you that you can't do something, or aren't able. The first step to realizing your ambitions is maintaining a positive attitude. Don't ever be a slave to drugs or alcohol; otherwise, you become just another casualty of life. Substance abuse is an escape from reality. It may dull pain and anxiety, but it deadens the spirit, numbs the capacity for joy, and dampens the exhilaration found in confronting life head-on. Meet challenges with a clear mind, and you will discover what it really means to be alive. You are meant to shine and be victorious! Don't needlessly cripple yourself with destructive habits!

At times loneliness is a gift; it allows you to discover who you are. Solitude is a time for reflection; a time to cultivate the will to take action. Don't ever, ever, hold back crying! It is a release, and cleanses your soul. Don't forget to laugh. When I was going through rough times, the best antidote to despair was laughter. A good sense of humor lightens any load. I've always liked being the clown; don't be afraid to look ridiculous occasionally. Don't hate; hatred is the ultimate toxin. Learn to forgive others and forgive yourself.

Harness pain and negativity—channel their potent energy towards the realization of constructive goals. I nurtured a lot of malignant feelings throughout my life. I had anger towards others and towards myself. I often tortured my own soul, and liked it. But I overcame by putting these powerful emotions in the service of positive ends. Rage and insecurity became the fire that drove me to prove to the world that I wasn't "a nobody."

If there is one thing I have learned, it is this: I am meant to shine, and so are you! Your life is the outward expression of the attitude found inside your heart. Cultivate love and forgiveness in your heart, and love and forgiveness will come back to you. It is a choice. Regardless of the character of your surroundings, remain an independent spirit. The independent heart is always free to soar, bravely and with hope, into new horizons. A heart that is swayed by the negativity of others becomes hardened, heavy, and bitter.

Remember, If I Can Fly, You Can Fly. Let your spirit soar, so that one day you might be able to help another person to Never Give Up!!!

"THE WAY I WAS"
A Little History

I've written this book as a follow-up to my first, *I Will Never Give Up*, in which I unloaded the contents of my soul for all to read. I'd hoped that my confessional journey would inspire others who had undergone, or were currently undergoing, struggles similar to my own. The book was a reminder to never lose hope; to always keep in mind the knowledge that "this too shall pass."

One chapter in *I Will Never Give Up* was entitled "Lost in Religion". In it, I discussed my lack of faith in God and criticized many aspects of organized religion. Since publishing the book, I've become much wiser, and more appreciative of the role God has played in my life. Narrow-mindedness was keeping me from developing a healthy, mature perspective. I needed to view life with a different set of eyes. Instead of critical negativity, I needed a spiritual attitude that was more positive and life-affirming.

Since writing the words which fill "Lost in Religion", I've had some amazing experiences and spiritual epiphanies. My perspective on God has changed profoundly. I've reconsidered the blessings in my life; blessings that before I'd failed to attribute to Him. I'm now eager to revise my earlier statements. As I write this response to the doubts expressed by a younger, more skeptical Derek, I'm filled with an immeasurable amount of gratitude: for the breath of life, for the goodness around me, and even for the sad, troubled past I had to overcome. This book is a product of my new outlook on God, and my full awareness of His presence.

The first part of this book is made up of excerpts from *I Will Never Give Up*, including part of the chapter "Lost In Religion". It was written during a time of earnest doubt and disbelief. It reveals the limited and negative perspective with which I viewed God and faith. Throughout life, I'd fallen into certain spiritual traps on account of my trials and tribulations. They tainted my relationship with God. I blamed Him not only for all my problems, but for the entire world's problems. It didn't even occur to me that God was something much greater, much more magnificent, than a place to point my accusatory finger.

In the second part of the book, I share the many inspiring moments and epiphanies I've had since writing *I Will Never Give Up*. These experiences have given me a more mature, much broader idea of God. For years, I'd been carrying on my shoulders a ten-ton backpack; the oppressive burden of anger against God. My difficult past gave me a skeptical view on the reality of a loving God. It has been a great challenge for me to find respect and love for God. My heart was so hardened by anger! But I can no longer look at my life as having been cursed early on. I understand now that my early hardships were actually blessings.

It is my prayer that this book touches you. It is my prayer that you focus on God's miracles, big and small, instead of fixating on the negative things found in His creation. I hope that by revealing the ups and downs of my own spiritual growth, you may avoid the mental and spiritual anguish I endured by thinking the worst of God. I want to give hope to those spiritual journeyers who may feel helpless in their struggle to find meaning and purpose in their lives. I want them to know that God is there! He can provide the strength we need to overcome obstacles. He is the greatest ally in our mission to become the best we can be.

The Seeds of Doubt

This is the true story of my life. A life in which abuse, loneliness, and dark nights of despair rattled the bones of my body, drained the tears from my spirit, shattered my mind into a million fragments, and left me for awhile plodding through life as an empty shell, a lost and helpless soul. I have breathed the air of the unloved, and suffered deep wounds due to being abandoned by my mother and father at an early age. I have blamed myself for a past over which I had no control. My trust in people was displaced with hostility and anger. And yet, *my spirit would not be broken.* I have fought for survival in the name of love, powered by a dogged will whose voice never stopped telling me to NEVER GIVE UP!

I was a five year-old kid, and already a survivor of dreadful and disheartening events. I have never known my biological father, but learned from social service reports that he abused me as an infant. My stepfather was hardly any kinder. My mother, having given up on me, placed me in the County Social Services Foster Care System. She was desperate to be

5

rid of me. The saddest, most inexplicable part of this was that she kept my younger brother and older sister. I was devastated knowing I had been deleted from the family. I was motherless and fatherless.

I loved my mother, brother and sister, but my love for them wasn't enough to keep me in the family. She claimed she could not control me, and accused me of being a "devil." But I was the child and she was the adult. I am not to blame for the predicament I found myself in. That is life; it is unfair.

The shameful actions of parents will always be remembered by their children. I know, because that five year-old foster child still lives within me, constantly striving to be empowered, to make his insecurities my own. But I refuse to be a victim; I am a victor. I am stronger than my unworthy parents!

There is no question; the mental and physical strugles of my life have proved very difficult to overcome. They say the first five years of a child's life are the most critical to his or her development, and that children soak up everything they experience like a sponge. I agree. I have seen my own three children sponge both my strengths and weaknesses. Kids watch their parents, and mimic what they observe. The influence of my first five years contributed to many destructive behaviors throughout my life. I often wished I had been given away at birth, so that I wouldn't have had to endure the memories and night-mares which have haunted me these many years. There is always a lesson to be learned from adversity. I have learned many such lessons the hard way, but have found there is a light at the end of the tunnel, and that light is Hope. I believe in Hope.

I am just a real person who has had real struggles, and had to deal with them the hard way. I am not a doctor, nor do I hold a degree in psychology. I can't claim to have graduated from a prestigious university with a 4.0 G.P.A. I am not here to "fix" you or put your life together in the way I see fit. I am here to show you how I first identified, and then modified, my thought processes.

I believe unhappy thoughts lead to unhappy actions, with the end result being an unhappy life. We all want a happy life, and to achieve a peaceful state of mind. I believe that what you think you are or can be, you have the power to be. The challenge is to **become** the person you want to be. My credentials are relevant, credible and simple. They are "real life" tragedies and triumphant experiences. I am in touch with my inner self and thought that now, having overcome, I would take the opportunity to share my experiences; those experiences which I have survived, and how I have thrived in spite of them. We are all imperfect and sometimes choose to unwisely focus on our suffering. We become attached to our pain, making it a part of who we are. But there comes a time when we can no longer relinquish our minds and bodies to the victim mentality. We must become victors.

A person doesn't need a college degree to deeply touch another's soul. We are all human and feel emotions, whether it is fear, love, happiness, anger or sadness. People can make an impact on others in dramatic, life-changing ways, both negative or positive. Your life has meaning! Life is about continual learning and becoming wiser. I believe in turning disadvantages into advantages.

Where Are You God?

Here I was, a child desperate for love and affection, a scared little boy who was getting ready for what would be the longest ride of his life. I can't say I remember the drive to the orphanage, or the place where kids were stored, but I do remember not bringing along any toys. I remember the sun being out and the sky being blue. The day was pleasant, warm, and peaceful, in stark contrast to the foreboding anxiety that was raging inside me. I didn't know where I was being taken, only that this day would likely be the darkest of my life.

The "longest ride" eventually ended at a place I considered an orphanage. It was a big building with lots of space and rooms. I figured it was an orphanage because all I saw were homeless and unloved kids. Kids who were no longer wanted by their Moms and Dads. I could see the sadness and fear in their eyes, and imagined that same fear must be showing in mine. We were now disposable, kids who could be thrown away or tossed overboard, never to be loved or comforted by our parents again.

Seriously, who would have cared if we were drowned or burned to death? At this point, it was already like we were being buried alive. We were being killed, suffocated, by lack of love. We were now the county's worry, pain and nightmare.

My parents had given up! They were weak, and now I had to somehow become strong and survive. The memories and questions were killing me. I kept thinking, 'Where is my big sister?' I thought that surely she would come and rescue me because she loved me. I expected her to show up at any minute. But nobody came! Here I was, a helpless little five year-old boy, and my heart no longer beat for anybody but myself. Hope was lost for me at that point.

I don't even remember seeing my mother's eyes, or her giving me one final hug, or her even saying something as simple as "I love you Derek," or, "I will be back for you son." How could she not even give me a goodbye hug? She was the one who had placed both herself and me in this position. I was the son, paying the price for all of her bad choices. She could have at least said, "Well, take care Derek, I love you."

Or how about just a few basic words of tenderness and

encouragement? "You will make it through this Derek." Even something negative, critical, or hurtful would have been better than nothing: "I blame you for all of this," or "Derek, you are the devil," or "Derek, I hate you for what you have become," or "Derek, you forced me to do this, I blame you!" But NO, nothing was said at that moment, and the indifferent silence was more painful than any words could have been, no matter how angry or loveless.

I guess it wasn't like she was wishing me well as I went off to college. I'm sure she quickly got rid of me in order to avoid the emotional impact of her actions, of seeing herself throwing away her own blood, her selfish desire to choose her husband over me, her son. But as her blood son, I probably reminded her of past mistakes, of the regretful choice she made to start a romantic relationship with my biological father. I have no doubt my stepfather comforted her, and told her she was making the right choice in giving her son away. Even as a little boy, I was certain he had been the one pushing to give me away.

He broke up our family. I hoped that every day after he gave me up he lived a life of hell, and that when he died, hell would take him back. My Mom used to call me the devil, but as far as I could see, she'd married the devil. She got it all mixed up. Mother, you married the devil.

After she dropped me off, my little life as a boy who nobody could or would love began. At this time, even I wasn't able to love this little boy. Plagued with insecurities and doubts about my self-worth, I was now going to have to make a home here in hell. I was left alone with all the bigger boys, who just stared at me like wolves salivating at the thought of feasting on a weak, vulnerable little lamb. I was the proverbial sheep being led to the slaughter.

I was very alert and very scared. Very, very, very scared! A woman took me into another room and showed me around. It technically wasn't an orphanage, but there was very little difference between an orphanage and whatever this place was. Besides, what difference did it make? It was an imposing, overwhelming, cold, impersonal and institutional building. There was no love here. This was a place of pain and ghosts. We were throwaways or misfits. Possibly we were angels who nobody recognized as such, but that could hardly have occurred to us at the time. This was to be my new home while a new family was being prepared for me. I didn't know who or what kind of people might invite me to share in their life. Or for that matter, if anybody would want me at all. I cried from loneliness and fear.

I remember thinking that my Mom would of course be coming back for me. I could care less about my stepfather, but I trusted that my mother's love would override whatever other concerns she had. I felt a deep hatred for my stepfather. He had taken my Mom away from me. If she didn't come back, I placed the blame squarely on his shoulders.

The older boys antagonized and threatened me, trying to push my limits. I got angry and taunted them back, so one of the boys pulled out a toothbrush with the end sharpened for use as a weapon. I ran for my life. I thought I was going to die. I knew what death was even at a young age. According to the county reports, I had a kind of morbid fascination with death. Later that night, when it got dark, I grew even more frightened. It became obvious that if my mother was going to come back for me, it wouldn't be any time soon.

We slept in what appeared to me like a giant classroom with a bunch of beds placed in it. It was some kind of enormous warehouse for storing kids. I remember hearing lots of crying in the middle of the night, puncturing the silence. Other kids were missing their Moms and Dads, brother and sisters. Where were mine? I wondered why my brother and sister got to stay with our mother and I was stuck here in this sad, terrible place. Why was I rejected and deleted from the family? Was I special somehow, or was I just a piece of garbage? Why couldn't I just be a normal kid like others? A kid who had a family? Why didn't anyone love me?

God, Help Me! I Am Searching For You!

This chapter is from my previous book. I wanted you to see where I was spiritually before you read the remainder of this book. "I may be disappointing my family and friends with the truthfulness of what I'm writing. But I feel the only way for me to grow is by being completely honest about myself and my limited religious beliefs. My intent is to be completely real regarding my faith. I have to be honest so that my words can help other's who may think as I do. I am not here to be politically correct or water my feelings down. This is the truth that I must answer to every night, when the lights go out and I am alone with my conscience. I have been involved in religion most of my life, and have taken all the necessary steps in order to build my religious faith, but yet, I have not felt it. I have been told that if you go through the motions and make a daily habit of submitting yourself to religious faith, it will grow and blossom. I am sad to say that my faith has not really grown, and the pressure of try- ing to build my religious belief has mentally wiped me out.

How does one really know the absolute and physical truth of God or God's love? Sure, I've heard all the stories in the Bible and other religious books, but I just don't know what to think about it. I know that the Bible teaches great principles of how to live life with a more peaceful state of mind. It teaches us how to forgive, not to judge, to love and turn the other cheek. It tells the wondrous miracles of Jesus and the love he had for mankind. The Bible shows that he was a great example for others; how much he sacrificed, how much he was abused, yet still loved all. I read the Bible almost every day with my family because it set forth great guidelines for living a righteous life, and gave examples of choosing right actions. It also divulged the consequences for those who made bad choices.

Even though my faith is limited, I still enjoy learning the lessons of the Bible; but I often feel like Neo in the hit movie *The Matrix*, always searching for the mysterious "force behind reality," which in my case is God. Once in a while, I question whether God is really out there, and just rely on what everyone else says they feel about Him; their claims that they are certain their prayers have been answered. This keeps my faith going, and keeps the hope alive that one day He will answer my own prayers. For most of my life, I've been searching and praying every day, but it usually feels like I'm praying to the wind. I've never felt that God has answered me. I have acted earnestly, and believed faith would come by participating in spiritual practices.

I have always struggled with the suffering of the innocent. I can only imagine the faith a mother has when her child is diagnosed with cancer and has only a few months to live. She is probably praying with utter sincerity and devotion to God, asking that He not take her child away. Yet, often the child passes on. I also feel for the starving children throughout the world, when they pray for food that doesn't come.

Faith arises from particular situations, and is the method whereby a person seeks comfort during times of need and suffering. I think we all pray for the needy at times in hopes that God will show His compassion toward those who suffer. When relief and mercy do not come, the value of faith is questioned.

Life is confusing, and I don't always know what to believe. There are only a select few who can enjoy unwavering faith. They never question anything. It is like they have a knowledge others do not. I believe some people are directly connected to God, and it is beautiful to see this connection. But I am not one of those people. I would like to have that unwavering faith. Anyone who has suffered or gone through bad experiences either strengthens their faith or lets it fade away. I continually try to strengthen it day by day. But just because I don't have this unwavering faith doesn't mean that I don't believe in God. I am always going through the process of questioning my faith, and I will never give up trying to find it.

While a lot my friends and family can give inspiring testimonies about God and how He has answered their prayers, I myself feel nothing. I have carried the burden of feeling unloved by God my entire life. I do feel blessed, only not from a religious perspective. Rather, blessed as a person who appreciates happiness and loves existence. I have got to believe that there is a God, and this God created this world, the universe, galaxies, every living person, animals, and organisms. But when I consider the billions of people and the great marvels of this world, all created by God, I feel so small and insignificant in relation to Him that it bars me from feeling connected to Him.

I feel I am open to inspiration but it doesn't come in a religious or faith-building way. It comes through intuition and openness of mind. My inspirational moments are the closest I have ever been to God. I give Him credit for putting those thoughts in my mind. I then take action on them. Despite not feeling a powerful connection with God, I still wonder why God allowed me and so many others to be born into such stunningly dysfunctional environments? Why did I have to suffer more than most kids?

Is there truth out there? Will God ever show me that He loves me and understands me? Why is God silent with me? Have I become too cold to feel His love and spiritual warmth? Is it too late for me to be saved?

I pray for truth, but I've never heard the "still, small voice" that provides a convincing answer. Nor have I heard the thundering voice of God speaking to me. I can wish and hope for things unseen, but I have never known anyone who has come back from the other side to tell me their way is the only way and the only truth. Even with all the suffering in the world, church leaders still say "Ask and ye shall receive." I have come to realize that I can no longer entertain this "wish upon a star" frame of mind. It encourages spiritual weakness, and puts rescue outside of our own hands and beyond our control. My understanding of free will leads me to conclude that God does not intervene in our lives, and does not grant wishes. If it were otherwise, all the wishes of all the people suffering would be granted, and this appears to not be the case. If God does intervene but hasn't been willing to do so in these cases, that would imply He is playing favorites.

I am no more important than the starving children of the world. Why would he answer my prayers, while theirs go ignored? The plain and simple fact is that if you want something done, you have to do it yourself. I have always lived according to this belief, and have enjoyed great success. What I sow, I reap. The responsibility is all mine. Free will, as I understand it, is a gift that empowers us and calls us to action."

God, Will You Protect Me?

I have had a recurring nightmare since I was a little kid. It has caused me great confusion, as it deals with the possibility that God never loved me. This nightmare still haunts me, even in my adulthood. I've always wondered whether there was some truth to this nightmare. If not, why have I kept having it for all these years?

I am a little kid, about five years old, running through a field of yellow grass. A man is chasing me. The sun is going down and darkness quickly approaching. I can't see who the man is, but he is angry with me and I am very scared. As I run, I keep looking over my shoulder to see if he is gaining ground on me. I can feel my heart beating so strongly in my chest. It is getting darker.

Over a rolling hill, I see a church with a large steeple and huge stained-glass windows. I run to it. I am very small in comparison to the church. I pull the enormous double-doors open and run inside. There is a loud bang behind me as the doors close. The church is dark, lit only by the weak flame of a few candles. The man

21

is still chasing me. I can hear him screaming outside, so I run around the church trying to find a hiding place. The many grim statues are scary. They're staring at me, as are the faces in the stained-glass. The walls and floors are dark grey, and seem to be made of stone and cold cement. The air is chilly. It is not a warm or comforting place. I do not feel protected. I do not feel safe. I haven't found a hiding place. I continue to run. The building is so very large.

I run down to the end of a long hallway and try to open the set of doors there. They are locked. The man chasing me is now inside the church. I can hear him screaming. Suddenly, in a very low, deep, and evil voice he calls me by my name. I do not recognize his voice. I have never heard anger like the anger I hear in his voice, nor have I ever been this scared. My heart is pounding intensely.

I really believe I am going to die. I hide behind a large statue in the corner and see a dark figure opening the doors with ease, as if they were opened by some demonic power. The sound of the doors crashing open echoes through my ears. My frightened breath is coming in gasps, and I fear the man can hear me taking in air. I wonder if this will be the final moments of my life.

I sneak out from behind the statue, going down the hallway and into a big room with lots of pews. I hide behind one of them, but it doesn't feel safe. It seems as if all the many statues in the walls are staring at me in order to give away my hiding place. It's as if they are conspiring with this man; are on the same side. I notice that all the statues have wings, as does the man in the shadows. I can see the silhouettes of his wings as he walks around in the dark. As I lay there sweating profusely in the darkness, my heart nearly beating out of my chest, I know that my life depends on my being silent.

And then, with no resolution, I wake up with the vague and disturbing feeling of being unsafe, that nobody will come to my rescue, that there is nobody protecting me. Having analyzed this dream time and again throughout my life, I have come to the conclusion that there is something either about Church or God that doesn't sit right with me. I feel no love or protection. I do pray every day and read the Bible. I do all the things my foster family and church has taught me to do, but feel I am still unable to enjoy intimate, meaningful communication with God. I have felt alone, in the spiritual sense, for so many years.

GOD SAVE ME!

Child abuse is incomprehensibly hurtful and damaging to a child. I have been on the receiving end of child abuse and it has haunted me throughout my life. I'm not talking about a spanking once in a while. I am talking about inflicting severe pain on a child with the intent to cause physical trauma. I am talking about an out of control adult inflicting horrific pain on their own flesh and blood, a helpless little kid. Most mothers and fathers would do anything for their children, even die for them, but some soulless mothers and fathers are more than willing to hurt their kids mentally and physically.

I still remember very vividly one of the most horrific abuse incidents which ever happened to me. It is so embedded in my soul that it feels as if it just happened yesterday.

It was a sunny day in California. The year was 1975. I was a kindergartner. I was a curious and tough five year-old boy. My mother, stepfather, half-brother, half-sister and I lived in a two story townhouse. There was nice green grass in the front of the house. When you walked inside, you saw the dining room and kitchen on the right and the family room on the left. In front of you was a staircase with a black iron banister leading to the bathroom and the bedrooms. The bathroom was located at the top of the stairs. The house was furnished and I remember the wood being very dark with big lamps made out of clear orange textured glass.

On the table and kitchen counter there would always be empty yellow Coors beer cans. I remember seeing lots of yellow Coors beer cans in those days.

I would often be outside playing in the tunnels under the main road overpass near our house. As a kid I called them tunnels but as an adult looking back, they were big storm drain pipes that went under the street.

I am amazed that my Mom would let me wander and play over there at such a young age. I would love to hang out there and throw rocks at the metal siding of the pipes. When the rocks would hit, it would make a cool high-pitched noise that would echo through the tunnels. It would be exciting to sit under the overpass and hear the cars go honking by overhead. Sometimes I would find dead rats in there and lots of interesting junk. At times, adults would walk through, using the tunnels as a shortcut. Older kids would sometimes hang out in them. If I was alone, the tunnels would scare me a little, but I was tough and showed no fear.

One day, it was starting to get dark and I decided to head home. When I entered the townhouse, I could hear an argument going on between my mother and stepfather. I also remember a few yellow Coors beer cans. My mother asked me to do something. I defied her and said, "Screw you!" but really using the F-word. This wasn't the first time I had said these words to my mother. In fact the F-word was one of my favorite words at that age. But this time when I said it, my mother snapped, apparently having had enough of my disrespectful language. With anger in her eyes, she grabbed my arm and tried to pull me up the stairs. I resisted and fought back. I was yelling and she was yelling. It was very chaotic.

I was hitting her and she was hitting me, but eventually she overpowered me. She pulled me up the stairs to the bathroom and physically forced me to the sink. While holding me there, she turned on the hot water full blast, running it until the steam was rising profusely. She kept yelling at me, screaming that I was

never to use the F-word again, telling me how bad a
kid I was. She emphasized how terrible a kid I was
over and over again. I remember her yelling at me
uncontrollably. I think she must have totally snapped.
What she did next was incomprehensible. She
restrained my body and forced my tiny left hand under
the scalding hot water.

I was screaming, out of control and trying to pull my
hand out of the water. It hurt so much as she held it
there. I screamed "Mommy stop, Mommy stop!" I
was crying so loud, it hurt so much. I could not
believe my own mother was doing this to me. It was
like my life was flashing before my eyes and my
whole body was shutting down. It was like she never
heard me. I then yelled "Mommy, you're hurting me,
it hurts mommy, let me go, I love you." I tried to get
away but she looked at me with intense anger and said
I was a bad kid.

I thought I could get away, that I was stronger than
her. But I couldn't. I was only five years old. I was
helpless and completely at her mercy. The skin on the
back of my left hand was burned off. I have had this
scar ever since, on my body, in my heart, and in my
mind. All the other physical abuse I could deal with,

but this particular incident altered me physically and mentally forever. This was the final ticker for the time bomb that was about to go off. I was no longer an innocent little boy. I was now overcome with a sense of shame and anger that would last for years. I realized I was no longer good enough and that I was not really loved. I felt worthless and unwanted.

I now hated my mother. I hated her for not sticking up for me, and for not loving me. I hated her for hurting me. I was her son. Hate is such a powerful word and I don't use it lightly, but if there are two people that I hated, it was my mother and stepfather.

I can't say that I hated my father because I don't remember him, but my mother was supposed to protect and love me. I recently discovered from the case files on me that my biological father brutally abused me during my first year as a baby. Can you believe that? The wording is "Brutally abused." This was my biological father. How evil is that? I stop here and ask God, "Why did you place me with this family?" Why God, are innocent children born into such terrible situations?" Born to drug-addicted parents, sexually abusive parents, physically abusive parents, and alcoholic parents. These people are so selfish! They can't

29

think beyond themselves or realize how they are hurting and stunting the mental growth of their child. I can't stand the fact that they put themselves and their addictions before their children. If the cycle is not broken, each generation only gets worse.

There are too many distractions nowadays, pulling parents away from their children. These children don't have the good role models who could help them break the cycle. Most of them will become a product of their environment. It is unfortunate, but a good many parents don't deserve to be parents. They don't deserve to be the caretakers of Heaven's Angels. Each child is born pure and precious. They only want to be loved and they want to please their parents. They don't know negative feelings or words until their parents start showing them what a negative word or feeling means, and the child eventually mirrors the parent's example.

Everything you do or don't do with your kid molds them. What was once a pure and precious little angel can turn into an uncontrollable and aggressive little monster. I know this because my mother thought I was a devil. Sons and daughters want and deserve love from their mother and father no matter what. It doesn't matter how mean their parents are. They just want attention and love. Even as children grow into adults, they still yearn for the love and approval of their parents. I always wanted and desired my mother's love. Even as an adult, I just wanted to be validated by her.

Let's face it, I was a mistake. I was never supposed to be born. I'm sure my mother was frustrated when she accidentally became pregnant by a man who had so many emotional problems, a history of violence, who was a thief and convicted felon. Now I understand people can change for the better after making bad choices, but only IF THEY WANT TO. It appears that my biological father was never going to learn and was doomed to be a loser. My mother had to be frustrated for putting herself in that situation, and was unable to live with the consequences: me. I felt that I was a mistake, and that she was going to make me pay for it every time I behaved badly. I couldn't believe my own mother would hurt me as badly as she did, or be so vindictive.

I remember the pain. I feel the pain. I smell the pain and I see the pain. Never will I forget the memory of what was done to that innocent little five year-old boy. It is difficult to really describe the feeling of the hot scalding water burning off the majority of the skin on the top of my left hand. You could literally pull off parts of my flesh. It was awful!

I remember how angry my mother was. I wondered why I received this new kind of punishment. I kept asking, why has my mom hurt me so bad? I remember looking up at my mom and seeing her reflection in the mirror, the intense look she had, she was so focused on hurting me and taking out all of her frustration. No wonder I was diagnosed as emotionally disturbed or a "bad kid." I was a product of my environment.

This particular abusive event has followed me throughout my life. It has literally haunted me every time I take a shower. Before I get into the shower, I'll test the water with my hand to make sure it isn't too hot. Every time I touch the water, it automatically takes me back to the moment when my mother held my hand under the scalding water. It was uncontrollable. I could not block it out of my mind. I just lived it over and over every day of my life. It was like a broken record, constantly repeating over and over again. I had to make sure the water wasn't hot. I would look at my left hand and remember the skin burnt off and the pink color that showed beneath. I would also recall this horrific event every time I washed dishes, got into a hot tub, or washed my hands. If the water even had the possibility of being hot, I would recall the awful memory of being burned. I have thought about what my mother did to me every single day of my life, ever since the day it occurred.

I believe this was the greatest obstacle to me attaining complete happiness with myself at an early age. This unhappiness followed me everywhere. Anger would flow through my heart, then sadness. Every day I had to relive that experience, and it would put me in a negative frame of mind. If I could not get over it quickly enough, this negativity would color my entire day, affecting others around me.

Another unfortunate event happened to me when I was about five years old. I sometimes had a problem wetting my bed, or if I was mad at my parents I would pee on their things. That was my way of telling them I didn't want to be treated the way they were treating me. If I wet my bed the night before, my stepfather would become very angry with me. So he'd pull me over to the toilet and force my head into the bowl. He would stand over me and push my head down, forcing me to stay there. Now I didn't ever come close to drowning, but it wasn't a nice thing to do to another human being. He was treating me like a misbehaving dog or animal. He probably considered me an animal. He did not like me. I was the middle child, putting major pressure and stress on his marriage to my mother. He had his own son, the youngest, and I was now the bad seed. I'm sure he was nice to me in the beginning, at least until he won my Mom over.

Well this one time when he was sticking my head into the toilet, my mother heard the commotion. He was yelling at me about peeing my bed, telling me how angry he was. My Mom told him to stop holding my head down. There was a huge argument, and in the heat of it all, as he was forcing my head into the toilet, she grabbed my left hand and yanked my arm back. She yanked it so hard that she caused shoulder damage. I cannot tell you if it was dislocated, or if something was ripped or broken, but it was so painful that she made me a sling to hold my arm up. Years later, I still have pain in my shoulder, and it always rests higher than the other one. Every morning I have to try and force my bad shoulder down and stretch it out so that it's comfortable throughout the day.

At least after that day, my stepfather stopped putting

my head in the toilet. Abuse is hard to live with, but fortunately I am a fighter. I am a Victor who has set his mind free. Life isn't fair. The only thing I can control is my attitude and outlook on it. My philosophy and motto are simple: I WILL NEVER GIVE UP!

I started writing poems and songs when I was a senior in high school, soon after my brother and sister were killed. I was flooded with doubts about me being loved, and questioned my own ability to make the choices which would secure me a better life. My songs became a collection of the recurring thoughts that kept going through my mind. I found it very helpful to turn my emotions into art, to have an expressive outlet for them, so that I could then analyze them and see if they were making any sense, and whether or not they exposed certain negative or destructive tendencies. And if so, whether my artistic expression also revealed a way to overcome them.

I have never liked death or goodbyes. I have lost a foster brother seven years older than I, who I considered my brother, and my blood sister who was ten years older and a good friend of mine when I was in high school. I was sixteen years old when I found out that my blood sister was shot and killed by her brother-in-law, in some jealous rage over her filing for a divorce. She was shot in the head. This was on Mother's Day. She left behind two very young children. I had not seen or heard from her since I was five years old. When I was sixteen, I decided to write her a letter and she eventually wrote me back. She wanted to come and visit me. I wrote her back, never to hear from her again. My mother wrote to tell me the sad news of her death. I remember her being so gentle and loving to me. I hadn't seen her since I was put into a foster home. Eleven years later, I was brokenhearted to learn her life had been so brief on this Earth, and that we'd never be able to rekindle our relationship. It is unfortunate that we can never again enjoy the closeness we once shared.

My good friend in high school, and fellow soccer teammate, was killed for no reason. His father took a shotgun and killed him and his little sister while they were sleeping, then turned the gun on himself. I was in shock when the news circulated through school. I remember crying from the realization that life could be taken away at any point. It was unbelievable to think that just the day prior, I was playing soccer and joking around with him, and then the next day he was gone forever. He was a great guy, and I sorely missed him.

One of the most painful deaths was the loss of my foster brother. I was seventeen years old. He had his pilot's license and decided to fly some of his friends out for a weekend of fun. While they were flying over the Sequoia and Kings Canyon National Park, something went wrong and the plane crashed. He and a couple of his friends were killed. There was only one survivor. It was awful.

My foster Dad did not allow me to see his body and I am thankful because I would not want to remember my brother in this way. I would rather think of how great a brother he was. He was so accepting of me joining his family. I remember when I moved into the new foster home, he was in the garage working, and he spoke kindly to me. He taught me how to ride motorcycles and took me camping. He was definitely an important role model in my teenage life.

I found out he died when I came home at one in the morning after having been out dancing with some friends. My foster Mom and Dad were crying. I asked them what was wrong and they told me my brother had been killed in a plane crash. I was in state of unbelief. I could not believe my buddy was gone and that I wouldn't see him again in this lifetime. He had just gotten married the year before and had a lovely wife. I remember camping with them and the fun times we had.

After I heard of his death, I locked myself in my room for three days. I cried and cried. He was the only brother I had ever felt close to. I remember getting really mad at God and asking him why He'd taken away my sister and brother. One of my favorite movies at that time was *The Lost Boys*. It was about a group of young, rebellious vampires, free to do whatever they wanted. There was a new guy wanting to belong to their clique. I felt like that guy, a rebel and wanting to belong.

My brother made me feel like I belonged. He made me feel like I was his "real" brother. There was a song on the soundtrack called "Cry Little Sister," and I played that song over and over for many days. There was one line in particular that always stuck with me: "Come to your brother, thou shall not die....love is with your brother." I felt connected to my brother through this song. I was lonely. I now didn't have an older brother to take me motorcycling or camping, or for just hanging out with at his house. I remember thinking, "Well, now it's my turn to step up and fill the shoes of my older brother, and become the best brother I can be to my little foster brothers and sisters." Those were big shoes to fill, and I never could replace him. I grew up being a rebel and was completely rebellious throughout my teenage years. But after these deaths I began to recognize that death was a very real thing. People were dying all around me. It took my brother's death to wake me up. I had thought I was invincible. I can't tell you how many times I got in fights, but it was a lot.

As a teenager I had a problem with authority. Even as a little kid, I did not respect or trust authority. I started to really evolve into a good person when my brother died. It really hit home that I was no longer invincible and that I needed to get myself together. The death of my brother was what really started me on the road to personal change. I finally took ownership of my life and started to make better choices His death taught me that life was immeasurably valuable. I remember going to a three-day therapy seminar on how to move on from your problems and let go of your past. It was helpful, and laid the foundation for understanding myself and others.

So why am I writing all about death? Because your

life is so very precious. It is irreplaceable. You are the only person that can make it valuable. You can live your life or take your life away. You have the free will to make your life the way you want it to be. There are no excuses. I have seen how life takes away from the young and the old. Death does not discriminate. You cannot get your life back when you die. Life is not like a video game where you get to restart it and try again. Life is invaluable and cannot be bought back. All the money in the world will not buy your life back or the time that you have wasted. The most delicate and precious thing you have on this Earth is the limited amount of time you have to make the best of yourself and make a positive impact on other people.

It's easy for some to attribute all their successes to God. But in the darkness and silence that sometimes overcomes me, when I must give an honest assessment of my life and answer to my conscience, I don't always share with others the conviction that God is responsible for our victories in life.

Let me end on this note. I give God credit and thank Him for letting me live another day, for giving me the air to breath. I also thank Him for giving me three beautiful children. I do believe we have a soul or spirit that will one day live beyond this Earth, and I hope that in the end this spirit will reside in a place called Heaven. Perhaps one day I will feel the connection with God that others do. If that day comes to pass, I may have to retract everything I have written on the subject of God. And believe me, if that day comes, I will be more than happy to do so!

TRANSITIONS:
FROM DISLIKING GOD
TO LOVING GOD.

As you can see, my perspective on God was tainted because I blamed Him for every bad thing that happened to me. I felt like He never stuck up for me, and never helped make things between my family and me work out. With every mounting disappointment, I became more and more convinced He was not helping me work though my struggles. He was never there when I needed Him most. I no longer feared God, and secretly couldn't stand Him. I came to despise Him and the church leaders who claimed to represent Him. I was not reverent in church. I did not submit to God, and was out of control, even while on a church mission in Australia.

The anger I harbored toward God for separating me from my mother and siblings followed me throughout my life. It never went away. Even though I'd gone

43

through some awful abuse in her household, I still wanted to be with my Mom. Even though she thought I was possessed, at times even accusing me of being the devil, I still wanted her to hold me. This unfulfilled yearning tore me apart for years, messing with my head, heart and soul. As a young boy, I'd planted the seeds of hatred for the God who'd created me.

I blamed God for taking away my sister, and the close friends who were killed. I couldn't find comfort in believing God loved me. As sad situations kept arising, I became very comfortable swearing at God and cussing Him out. Sometimes, I'd try to get a rise out of God by teasing Him, to see if He even cared enough to respond. When I would pray and He didn't respond, I would let him have a piece of my mind. Even as I grew into adulthood, it was not unusual for me to challenge God. I'd always had problems with authority, and to me, God seemed like just another hypocritical authority figure. I didn't like anyone trying to control my life, and God was the ultimate controller, taking people away from me in terrible ways.

I hope the first section of this book demonstrated the limited and limiting way I used to think. I was completely lost. I was looking at God from a very narrow and immature perspective, not with the open-minded-ness demanded by faith. I am no longer that person. It's amazing how quickly a person can change.

The experience that led me to reconsider my relation-ship with God, and rethink my beliefs about His indif-ference, occurred on July 4th, 2008. I now consider this my personal Independence Day. It was a beauti-ful, sunny afternoon. My family and I were hosting a BBQ for some longtime family friends, another fami-ly with children around the same age as my own. Everyone had been playing in the pool, an above ground tank approximately four-and-a-half feet tall by eighteen feet wide. To get in the pool, swimmers had to climb a ladder up over the rim, then jump down into the water. Beside the pool was a trampoline. All seven children—Ozzy, Monte, Rebekkah, Solomon, Elijah, Remi and Ellie—were jumping and splashing around, having a great time.

After a while it was time to eat. We rounded up the kids to take a break. After a great 4th of July meal, our friends' three year-old daughter Ellie and my daughter of the same age, Remi, wanted to go back and play in the water. They asked their Moms if they could, press-ing them with pleas. The mothers said yes, but the requirement, as usual, was for them to wear their life-jackets. These jackets, specially built for children, had a buckle strap for running through a child's legs so parents could make sure the jackets were well-secured. After patiently waiting to be strapped into their jackets, off the two girls went. They were chatting and giggling, best friends, and the cutest little young ladies you've ever seen. This was their big day to hang out together, enjoying the cool water and warm weather.

The rest of us remained at the table enjoying the cook-out, only twenty-five feet from the pool. We were caught up in conversation, eating and laughing, having a great time, not imagining that right beside us tragedy was about to strike.

Bad things happen quickly. Only a few minutes had gone by when we heard our friends' nine year-old son Elijah yelling "Mom! Help!" Elijah had been jumping on the trampoline when he'd heard my girl Remi yell for Ellie: "Ellie, Ellie, Ellie!" Leaping off the trampoline, Elijah ran to look over the poolside. He saw Ellie underwater, laying flat on the bottom. Knowing there was something seriously wrong, he jumped over the rim into the water. Diving down, he brought Ellie up into the air, yelling "Mom! Help!" We heard his frightened, alarmed cry loud and clear. With the instant rush of adrenaline born of fright, we jumped up and ran toward the two children.

Ellie's mother Heather immediately grabbed the limp, lifeless body of her young daughter, pulling her over the side of the pool. Ellie was completely blue. Her face, lips and body. I've never seen this quality and shade of blue before. It was heart-wrenching to look upon this beautiful little girl in such horrible condition. Mucus was pouring out of her nose and mouth. She was completely still and unresponsive. I felt hopeless.

Heather laid Ellie down on the grass as I desperately dialed 911. As I was on the phone with the emergency dispatcher, Heather knelt in the grass, turning Ellie over onto her stomach so the water could run from her lungs. The 911 operator asked if Ellie had a pulse. Checking, Heather determined she did not. Relaying her instructions through me, the operator told me to have Heather begin CPR. Heather bent over, and prying Ellie's lips apart, started breathing into the girl's mouth, again and again. Ellie wasn't coming to life. The girl's father Will stood beside the terrible spectacle, in complete shock and utter disbelief, watching aghast as his wife tried breathing life into the lungs of their beautiful child.

Nothing was happening, but Ellie's mother continued CPR, when suddenly my wife held her hands to the sky over little Ellie and her mother. She proceeded to say the most powerful, impassioned prayer I'd ever heard. She pleaded with God to save this little girl. I was stricken by this unbelievable sight. I'd never seen my wife so intensely petitioning the Lord for help. God must have heard her prayer. Ellie's eyes opened for just a split second before rolling back into her head. Her mother cried "Come on Ellie!" Then her father: "Come on Ellie!" Then we all said it, pleadingly: "Come on Ellie!!!" We were holding onto our last bit of hope, begging her to come back to us.

Heather showed incredible strength, keeping herself admirably under control while she continued mouth-to-mouth. Hands still up in the air, my wife continued praying. Then it happened again. Ellie's eyes slowly opened, then rolled back in her head. "Come back, come back," we cried. We could sense life returning to her body, to us. She and her mother were both fighting for her precious life. Eyes still closed, drifting in and out of consciousness, Ellie started coughing.

We heard the ambulance and fire engine close by, their sirens blaring through the otherwise quiet day. Heather swept Ellie's still-limp body up in her arms and dashed carefully through our house, down our street to meet the vehicles. Handing Ellie over, the emergency crew immediately hooked her up to oxygen and drove off as quickly as they'd come, Heather sitting beside her daughter in the back.

Will and I briefly stayed behind and interviewed with the police officers who'd arrived. We then hopped in my car, and I steadied my nerves for the drive to the hospital. As long as I live I will never forget what Will said to me on that long and intense drive.

Will and Heather were known as a very spiritual, very religious couple, active in their church. We'd had many conversations together concerning my thoughts on God, my doubts and slanders. They were both familiar with my negative views on Him, attributing them, as I did, to my difficult past.

Driving to the hospital, Will and I were both in shock, and still very emotional. He turned to me then, and

49

said something that was so unexpected, so profound, that it hit me with the force of the Almighty God.

"Derek," he said, "I want you to know, that if God takes away my little baby, I will *praise* Him, I will *praise* Him."

The passion infusing his words, the utter sincerity in his voice, made my eyes tear up. It was amazing to witness this man's faith, his unshakable love of God, his absolute trust. It was a very eye-opening and revealing moment.

I knew that, personally, I would have reacted precisely the opposite way. I would have been mad at God, and cursed Him. I saw very clearly that since childhood I'd developed the reflexive habit of blaming God for every bad thing that happened in my life. The angry resentment would be doubled when, after praying for Him to fix my problems, He didn't. It was the "broken record" playing and secretly repeating in my head for years: "God is to blame, God is to blame, God is to blame." Because of my tainted past, my first thought as we drove to the hospital was that God was trying to hurt me again.

As I said, this July 4th was my Independence Day. I was liberated from my habit of blaming God. I was amazed! Here Will wasn't even thinking about blaming God in the event that his baby girl didn't make it. He maintained complete faith, still loving and respecting God in the midst of this tragedy. I needed that ability.

The drive to the hospital felt eternal. The atmosphere in the car was thick with distress from not knowing the outcome. Finally getting there, we rushed into the emergency room, trying quickly to find out where they'd taken Ellie. The hospital staff did not allow anyone but family or clergy inside Ellie's room, so I remained in the waiting room anxiously awaiting details. When Will got into the room he discovered Ellie was still unable to breathe on her own, and was still hooked up to oxygen. Lab tests revealed that she had water in her blood and lungs. She was in critical condition.

Will came out into the waiting room and told me the details. He was very emotional. I held him in my arms as he broke down crying. He told me that the doctors insisted Ellie be transported immediately to the Children's Hospital an hour away. I left my good friends in the care of their church pastor and went home to be with my family in their astonishment and grief. My wife and I cried and pleaded to God through prayer that He spare little Ellie, that He let her live and grow into adulthood. We could barely sleep that night as we awaited any word from Will and Heather on how Ellie was doing. It was a long, restless night, and we heard nothing.

The next morning was equally draining as we anticipated an update. Fearing the worst, hoping for the best. Finally the phone rang. It was Ellie's parents. They told us she could now breathe on her own and was alert, but not yet talking. We didn't dare bring it up, but we feared Ellie might have brain damage due to her oxygen deprivation. We just kept praying and crying, crying and praying. My wife and I kept thinking, "How could this happen to us? We are very careful parents. We were only twenty-five feet away from the pool."

We hadn't heard a second update from the parents for hours. We kept calling their cell phone, wanting to know if any news was available. Finally getting hold of Will and Heather, they told us Ellie was starting to get better. She could speak a little, but nobody was sure about brain damage, or whether her personality would be permanently effected, or whether she'd still have the adorable mannerisms and quirks that made her such an endearing child.

Then at 8:30, the night of the following Saturday, there was a knock at our door. My wife and I were still emotional wrecks, but we answered, completely unprepared for what happened next. Here at the door was that adorable little angel Ellie saying "Hi!" along with her parents. My wife and I burst into tears right there at the door, bending over to take Ellie in our arms, hugging her with all our might, with love and profound relief. We next embraced Will and Heather, thanking and praising God. This was a miracle! There was no doubt about it. She made it, and in doing so, showed me the beauty and mercy of God. I now call her my little angel Ellie. She is a living miracle.

The doctors said it was unbelievable she'd recovered so quickly. They were mystified. All the water was out of her lungs and blood, and her little brain was perfect. She had the same personality and characteristics as she did before the drowning. No brain damage whatsoever was detectable.

As parents, my wife and I are so careful that we'd already had Remi learn how to swim in order to prevent possible tragedy. We found out that Remi had taken off her life jacket, and Ellie had done the same; but Ellie couldn't swim. Ellie watched Remi jump from the ladder into the pool with such carefree delight, she decided it would be a wonderful thing for her to do too. So she jumped, but just sank instead of coming up to the surface. It happened that quick!

Already impressed by Will's reaction to the emergency, I was further moved by his and Heather's church congregation, and the communal love they showed for little angel Ellie and her family. During the course of Ellie's stay in the hospital, they'd been constantly keeping their thoughts and prayers focused on this wonderful family. Then they offered any and all kinds of help and comfort during the uneasy time after Ellie's release. I'd previously been critical of any church, but after seeing how these wonderful, compassionate people reacted, I now believe the church is a great tool to help others come to and feel the love of God. It definitely made this anxious family feel more loved and secure in their faith. I have had to take a good look at myself lately, and have been thinking about going back to church, something I wouldn't have even considered doing for a long time. I'd love to be a member of a church that I feel comfortable in, that would take me and my family in as their own.

Even now, months later, I'm choked up by recollections of this intense day. As I said, it was my Independence Day, in that I was finally released from the bondage of negativity toward God. Having before blamed God for the painful circumstances I'd encountered in my life, I now understand that, in fact, God was protecting me all along. He was blessing, not cursing me. I finally shrugged off the ten-ton burden of hatred towards God that had been weighing me down for decades. I've always been an advocate for personal progress, and now believe without a doubt that He has a plan for me, and always has. Thank God for Independence Day! My faith is restored! Since that day, I've felt my life unfolding in new, inspiring ways.

My children felt like contributing to this book by expressing their feelings about the miracle of little Ellie.

My 8 year old son Monte wrote:
"When my friend's sister almost drowned, we were so sad. We were in my room crying. Then we stopped when my friend said, just think about the good things. My friend Elijah is a good friend. He saved his sister. My dad called 911 and the ambulance came. She was saved. God is who saved Ellie. Thank God that she is still alive. We are really thankful. God is great."

My 6 year old son Ozzy wrote:
"I am so happy that God saved Ellie. It is a miracle that she is alive. Little Ellie could have died but God saved her. Thank you God for saving her."

My 3 year old daughter Remi said:
"Ellie is my best friend. It made me sad to see her go in the ambulance. She is kind and beautiful. God Saved her."

It is humbling and inspiring to hear my own children give God the credit for saving little Ellie. I was wrong about God. God gives hope. I was inspired to write this book, showing Him and others that I realize now what I didn't before. God loves me. He does have a purpose for each and every one of us. All I needed was to really feel the power of God. He has always been there for me, but I had to approach Him in a new way. He never really gave me the answers I'd wanted, but I realize He was still looking out for me. Sometimes we might look through our eyes for God, and not see Him anywhere. But we have to rely on faith, not eyesight. My problem was expecting God, if He existed, to demonstrate His love in a way that could be seen with the eyes, not felt with the heart.

"Derek, I want you to know that if God takes away my little baby, I Will Praise Him, I Will Praise Him."

Those words forever changed my life. What if it had been my daughter who'd drowned? Would I have had the faith to praise God during the most horrific experience of a father's life? I'd never considered God in a positive way. In my immature outlook, God was little more than a grand old wish-granter. The relationship was simple: you ask, and God has a duty to provide. But God never seemed to grant me any of my wishes.

I have seen and heard other people eagerly thanking God for what they have, and for the struggles He helped them endure. But I never felt any particular sense of gratitude toward God. Reviewing my life, it appears clearly to me that I've never thanked Him. After hearing my friend's words, I chose to appreciate the Creator of Life. They say the older you get, the wiser you become. Perhaps life doesn't unfold this way for everybody, but I certainly feel like it has for me.

For the greater part of my life, I believed God never listened to me. I felt like He'd thrown me away in the same callous way my parents had. I felt all alone. Believers may occasionally feel solitude, but their isolation is alleviated by their faith in the presence of God. I couldn't enjoy that same comfort. I was just lonely. As a kid, I felt even more alone in church, when the congregation would collectively bear testimony to the truth of God. I might be in the middle of a few hundred people, yet the loneliness would settle coldly over me like snow. I had no connection with God. Yes, I would smile and agree with everyone else, pretending to give testimony. But doing so, if it fooled anybody else, certainly didn't fool me. I always envied the others at my church. They were all so lucky, and so loved by God.

I questioned God's existence. I tested Him by showing no appreciation. I would yell at Him, cuss at Him, mock Him. I would disrespect the church leaders. I would act out in His holiest places of worship, and laugh loudly during prayers. I certainly had no love in my heart for Him. I would justify it by saying, "God doesn't love me. If He did, He wouldn't let little kids like me suffer. Why should I love Him?" The only time I've even felt close to God in any way was during the birth of my children. But the feeling of intimacy with something miraculous wasn't sustained, and I soon reverted back to my normal patterns of thinking.

As a child, I had a rough time mentally, emotionally and physically. I never considered the possibility that God was helping by getting me away from a mother who didn't care for me, or want me around—who even accused me of being possessed by the devil himself. Thank God I got out of that house. Had I been raised in that place, I probably would have turned into a mental case, or ended up in prison, or even dead. My mother, father, and stepfather all did some horrific things to me, so I must give God the credit for taking me out of that situation. God was there in His triumphant glory, lifting me out of a bad home, and putting me in a foster home where the parents worked with me and loved me, even though I'd been wrongly diagnosed as mentally retarded.

I have played the victim role by constantly blaming

God. I had an angel's heart, but I was a confused and mislabeled little boy who could only communicate through rage and violence. This tendency followed me into my teenager years, as I became more self-destructive. I now realize that I wasn't a victim of God, I was a victor with God, and He wanted the best for me. Although during my successes I didn't feel close to God, I really believe He helped strengthen me without my asking.

For me, there are no convincing explanations as to why I'm where I am in life. The statistics are not good for foster children. A lot of prisons are filled with former foster kids, boys and girls who had no direction and were given up on. I think the Holy Spirit must have been inspiring me to make the right choice in tough situations, or to write a particular song, or to write this book. God is working through me, not as He does through a Prophet or Holy Man, but as a person who has gone through so much pain. He knows I can be an instrument for Him by spreading the message of Never Giving up on God's Love. I am so appreciative that I am alive and living.

After my sister was killed, and not long after my stepbrother, I needed hope. This at a time when I was failing school, getting into trouble, and trying to figure out who I was as a teenager. It was so easy to lay these accidents on God's shoulders. I hadn't even thought to look at their deaths in a different way. I now don't believe God was determined to hurt Derek by taking the people he loved away from him. I can't explain death, or why people sometimes die before they live a long, full life. It makes me sad when young promising lives end so abruptly. It becomes unbearable for the people they leave behind. But I have also seen people strengthened in their faith after losing their child; they hold onto God even more.

Dr. Wayne Dyer said: "When you change the way you look at things, the things you look at change." Rather than get so upset and blame God for all the things that happened to me, why didn't I look at it as a way to get closer to Him? I chose to distance myself, and then wondered why He wouldn't answer my prayers or come to my aid when I called upon Him.

When I focused on the hate and the non-existence of God, I was continually poisoning my heart with negativity. I was fueling my body with poison instead of the light of my Heavenly Father. Rage clouded my judgment.

Will God Help You?

The answer is YES! Life is a journey. There will be doors of opportunity that open, and others that close. But one door that will always remain open is the door to your Heavenly Father. Whether you're struggling with an addiction, divorce, pain from the past or a financial crisis, this will be the one door you can always walk through. Through that door is inner peace, the knowledge that you're not alone in this crazy life. I rarely used that door because I figured it was more like the door to a jail cell. My pride and anger kept me from entering. I wrestle with the sad fact that I lost out on so much happiness and intimacy with God because of my hardened heart. But I look forward to the rest of my life, as I can now share God's message of peace to all who are struggling and feeling alone during a crisis.

When there are days that I struggle, I say, "God, help me find a way out of this. Bless me with the strength and knowledge that will carry me through this storm of life. I want to be an instrument for thee."

I recently discovered a long-forgotten journal entry

I'd made on October 14th, 1989. I'd written the entry soon after one of the most frightening experiences of my life. I'd forgotten about the incident, and the importance God had in my life that day. I believe He rescued me from death. After rereading this journal entry and revisiting the terror I'd felt, I was sad to see how quickly afterward I'd forgotten Him. I'd shut Him out, even after giving Him full credit for saving me. It's strange how we quickly change our beliefs and convictions. I'd been adamant in the belief that God didn't love me, but this journal entry showed a side of myself that I wouldn't see again for quite awhile.

The entry reads: "I went surfing at Pompanio Beach off Highway 1 today with my friend Allen. It was foggy and cold. When we got there and studied the swells, we noticed that the waves, six to eight feet high, were closing out on the right side. The left side was throwing good sets so we proceeded to paddle out. The water was cold when we got in. Thank goodness for wet suits. After we fought through the waves hammering down on us, we found a brief moment of peace, and were able to talk while waiting for the right wave to ride in. That's the great thing about surfing; you can just hang out in the ocean without a care in the world. Just you and the water and the guys you're hanging out with. No one can hear you. It's a great place for conversation.

"When done talking, we rode some waves in and repeated the cycle. It was a great day. I paddled out again, looking for the perfect wave, when I noticed my friend having a great time surfing about a hundred yards away. I finally made it out to the open sea, and was waiting to see if my friend would catch up to where I was. It was so peaceful out there by myself, just laying on my board thinking life couldn't get any better. When you become converted to surfing, it's almost like you become the ocean's protector. I had developed a love for these waters. As a surfer you come to appreciate the beauty of the ocean and the wave. Every ocean become a fantastic sight, and you look at it with a different pair of eyes, constantly admiring the rolling waves and their power as they crash against the beach. You come to realize that you are just a speck of sand on this sea. The ocean controls you and your ride, you don't control it. You come to have a deep respect for the power of the ocean.

"What happened next forever altered my relationship with the ocean. As I was kicking back on my board, I started drifting away to the right. I was being carried along rather quickly. Finding this a weird situation, I started paddling back to the left where I'd been before, but I couldn't get there. The ocean kept pulling me farther and farther out. I turned around and tried paddling towards the shore. The current wasn't letting me get back to the beach. I paddled harder and harder, without making an inch of progress. I continued to be pulled out. I was about 125 yards from the beach now, maybe more. I wanted more than anything in the world to be standing on that sand.

"I'd drifted out so far that I was behind the waves. They were forming in front of me. I needed them to form behind me in order to ride them in. I was getting scared. So what does a scared person do? They panic, and that's exactly what I did. I jumped off my board and started swimming towards the shore. This was precisely the wrong thing to do. Surfers don't go out with life jackets. They use their board as a flotation device. I tired out quickly, and still hadn't made any progress. I was no match for the power of the ocean. I grabbed my board (thankfully the strap was still attached to my ankle) and yelled out for help. I was stressing, becoming short of breath. No one could hear my screams, so I screamed louder. It didn't help.

"I was getting emotionally and physically worn out, so I started praying for God to help me get to shore. I was praying out loud with my eyes open, looking out for a wave that could carry me. Suddenly, I looked to my right and saw a giant hole in the ocean. It was a giant, funneling whirlpool, fifteen to twenty feet in diameter. The water was running in a circular motion down the hole. It seemed deep, and I was slowly being pulled towards it. Now I really started to panic. With whatever strength I had left, I paddled as hard as I could to get away. It wasn't working. It seemed destined that I be sucked down this hole to nowhere. I didn't want my life to end by drowning.

"Being pulled underwater is the worst thing that can happen to a surfer. When the waves suck you under, you're tumbling around disoriented in the churning water. You also have wave after wave crashing down on top of you, keeping you down and further disturbing the water. You don't really know which way is up, unless you can see the sunlight, or grab the leash to your board, which will always float up. There had been many times when I'd almost ran out of air beneath the water, struggling to find my way to the surface. "I was breathing so hard, almost hyperventilating. I was thinking the worst, that this was it. I am going to die.

I prayed to God one last time as I neared the edge of the whirlpool. There was nothing left for me to do, so I begged Him with all of my heart to help me. I was completely wiped out, the strength in my fatigued arms faded to its last. Then, when I had just given up all hope, a wave came suddenly as if out of nowhere, and carried me all the way in. I didn't even have to ride the wave in by standing up. I just laid on the board. When I got off the board, I was so exhausted I couldn't even walk. I just fell forward onto my face. Thank God for sand! My voice was hoarse from yelling for help. It was one of the scariest moments in my life. I was sure I was going to die, and that I had no control over my destiny.

"I know the only way I got out of this situation was because God heard my prayer. There was no explanation for that funnel hole, and no explanation for why I couldn't paddle back to shore. No explanation for the wave from out of nowhere that carried me to safety, all without any effort of my own. It was a miracle. This was one of those defining moments, showing the mercy and power of God. Was God testing my faith? Why was that hole there? I have never seen anything like that before. Needless to say, I have never surfed again, even though I loved surfing all the time.

I believe there was a greater force at work out there. Looking back, it seems like a struggle was taking place. On one side was an evil force that wanted me dead. On the other was God saving me from imminent death. Was I in the middle of a power struggle between good and evil? I'm glad that I was able to pray to God and that he helped me through this horrific and scary event."

As time went on, the memory of God helping me would fade. How quickly I forgot about the power of God! As my mind is now clear, I will never forget His power!

My trials, like yours, are just part of a journey towards eventual triumph. Victory is right around the corner. Maybe a minute or an hour away, a day or a week away, maybe even a year away. Regardless, hold strong and fight negativity with Faith. Faith in God will lessen the time it takes for your particular crisis to play out. I believe my lack of faith made me suffer more than was necessary. If I'd had faith in God's ability to strengthen me, and not been so focused on Him rescuing me, I would have prevailed much faster. I was trying to use God as a crutch, trying to make Him grant me my wishes during hard times. I didn't realize that what I should have prayed for was patience, energy, and knowledge. I should have prayed that He inspire me with the wisdom to find solutions.

I once heard a saying: "Don't talk *about* your problems, talk *to* your problems." To me this means stop complaining about all the strife in your life. Instead, tell yourself these struggles are not permanent. Talk to your problems and tell them it's time they start moving along.

I believe I'm right where I'm supposed to be in life. I no longer live in the past, filled with regret, blame, guilt and anger. I live in the present, surrounded by peace, love, family and happiness. We're all entitled to the good things in life. Ultimately, whether we have them or not is a choice we make. Changing the way we look at a problem is a choice. It was a choice for me to dislike God. It was a choice for me to place my faith in Him. We all have the blessing of God behind us. It is His strength that carries us to victory.

FORGIVENESS

After the "Ellie Incident", my view on God was forever changed. My perception of Him was much more clear-headed, not so clouded by previous history. With clarity came guilt. I realized I had done some real trash-talking about my God. When I was blaspheming and disparaging Him, I didn't think I was poisoning myself with the spiteful mockery, but I was. It all became so obvious. I felt guilty for not respecting the Creator of my life. I realized that I now had to have a heart-to-heart talk with God. This was a whole new level of communication. It'd been so long since I sincerely prayed. I kneeled on the floor in my closet, where I knew I wouldn't be interrupted. I bowed my head and crossed my arms reverently, waiting in silence. I gathered my thoughts on what I wanted to say to the Almighty God. Tears of shame started to swell up in my eyes. I opened them for a moment, then squeezed them shut, causing hot tears to roll down my cheeks. These tears were long overdue.

I started off my prayer by saying "God, please forgive me. Forgive me for what I have become in Your eyes. Please forgive me for the disrespect and mockery, for taking your name in vain all these years." I needed to get it all out, confess both to myself and to God the true nature of what I'd done, and let Him cast His righteous judgment upon me. What I felt next was not judgment, not harsh words, not sudden death or the cold shoulder of God. I felt only warmth and love. God didn't say anything to me, exactly. I didn't hear His booming voice reverberating through my head. But He did put peace in my heart, something I hadn't enjoyed for a long time.

You see, when you harbor negative feelings in your heart, you can still become successful in life. You can make money and friends. But it's hard to feel gratitude toward the creator of life, God. I was successful in my personal and financial life, but spiritually I was poverty-stricken. I still didn't believe in a God who loved me, a God who wanted to help me. God was still an adversary. When I was yelling, cursing, and taking His name in vain, I knew I was doing something wrong. But the more I did it, the less wrong it came to feel. Sacrilege became a habit. It became easier and easier to cut Him off and disrespect Him. The more I insulted God the further away I pushed Him. But the further away He became, the more I wished for intimacy with Him.

Even so filled with anger, I didn't entirely sever myself from God. I still went to church and tried to do the right thing. I just didn't care for Him as my God. I thought if I tried to follow His rules, He would miraculously call me by name one day: "Derek, you make me so proud!" I longed for something, some kind of grace, that I knew only God could provide, but I grew tired waiting for Him. Like an impertinent child I tried to chastise Him for not bending to my own needs and desires. What a patient God He is! After all these years of ill-will I'd shown Him, I knew He didn't judge me, or hold me accountable for all the things I said and did. But on my knees, crying in the closet, asking for his mercy, I only felt the peace of forgiveness.

As I finished up my prayer, I knew God did love me. I knew He'd been watching over me my entire life. I was certain of this. At times, when I picture Him looking down on me, I see sadness in His eyes. He sees me keep stumbling through my trials and tribulations. He sees me making mistakes and take the wrong path. I think of Him waiting for me to call on Him, saying "Heavenly Father, please help me find a solution! Give me the strength to fight my way through this trial!" I don't believe God was waiting for me to say, "Hey God! Get me out of this situation now!" I now know to ask for inspiration, guidance, and wisdom, so I can make the right decisions.

Instead of merely begging to be rescued, I ask for a change of perspective. God wants us to learn the lessons life has to teach. If we don't experience struggle, we aren't fully human. How do you become a stronger person? Not from constantly being rescued, but marching your way victoriously through the trenches. It gives me great pleasure knowing I have overcome a troubled past. If I had been rescued, perhaps I'd have taken a much different road in life. Maybe I would have been content with feeling like a victim. Maybe I would have never seen the value of developing personal strength and endurance. Maybe weakness would have led me to drug and alcohol addiction, or unable to resist a violent impulse.

Trials have made me stronger, period. I would not want to trade my problems for anybody else's. I wouldn't want to walk in anyone else's shoes, whether more comfortable or not. My shoes were designed for walking through my own problems. My shoes have carried me through some pretty chaotic journeys. My shoes and I have traveled through the thick of many storms. And now I'm able to buy some great shoes for these weathered feet! My new shoes are water-proof, storm-proof, and heat-proof! No way, no sir, I do not want to have on any shoes that are not my own. I am blessed for the problems I've had to overcome. I believe God gave me problems because He wanted me to overcome. God has a plan for Derek Clark.

As I get older, and hopefully wiser, God inspires me to be smarter, to value life more, and to share an important message. The message is that no problem is so big or so small, so simple or so complex, that you cannot ask Him for guidance. You just have to ask with true intent and a humble heart. Prayer doesn't secure you a fast-track pass to God and a bunch of easy answers. I don't believe He will completely deliver you from troubles without you doing your part. I believe He'll give you the strength and insight to deliver yourself from any particular problem. He is a strength and He wants to help you help yourself. I believe we're all here to learn lessons that are particular to our own life. Without these lessons, we remain souls stunted in our growth.

I no longer have animosity towards God. He has released me from the bonds of my own personal hell. He has helped me break the shackles of ego and pride.

He has given me the insight to know that my weaknesses one day will become my strengths. The strong rely on God! I am still here breathing on this Earth. I have a yearning to praise Him. I have compassion in my heart for my fellow men and women. God is now by my side. I have let Him in my heart.

BELIEVING IS MY CHOICE

So there I was with a hardened heart, feeling abandoned by God. But in reality, I had abandoned God. He was always there. I just got tired of looking for Him because it seemed like He never gave me anything I asked for. I felt unloved, when truthfully, I was losing my love for God. Looking back, do I really think God abandoned me in my time of need? The answer is NO. I believe my trials were a journey He sent me on, a rocky path toward discovering what He wanted of me, my purpose in life. Over the years, I often ventured off this rocky path, taking side-streets, detours, and dirt roads. I don't think I was lost during that time. I was only sight-seeing before returning to the main avenue, where I eventually found the way to spiritual awareness.

On my sight-seeing detours, I learned valuable lessons; sometimes painful, sometimes dangerous, and usually destructive. I was not worried about dying. I couldn't cry because crying was a symbol of weakness. I had to be tough, to show that nobody mattered to me, not even myself. I had to be popular by being the disrespectful one. Disrespectful of elders, authority, myself and God. There is nothing to be gained from blind and thoughtless disrespect.

On an early morning not too long ago, I had an epiphany while walking my dog. These particular words miraculously came into my head, and struck me with their power. My mind told me, "Derek, you can either choose to dwell on the good things about God, or you can choose to dwell on the bad things about God." I am completely guilty of dwelling on the bad things. Instead of focusing on the pretty flowers God created, I focused on the thistles and weeds. Instead of dwelling on the miracles which God had His hand in, I chose to dwell on the dirty and depressing things.

There is so much suffering in this world, it's often easier to see the negative. It is a choice to have an attitude of gratitude, just as it's a choice to have no appreciation for the Creator. Nowadays, I often think, why wouldn't someone want to believe in God? Belief in God brings so much hope, faith, strength and happiness. It produces a happier outlook on life. Compare this to the attitude of someone who doesn't believe in God, who is constantly trying to prove that God doesn't exist. This is sheer negativity! There is long-lasting happiness to be found in having faith. Why not have hope for an afterlife, or hope you will achieve the goal of getting into Heaven? Those who don't believe in God are usually on the defensive. This negativity completely colors their attitude. I have questioned the existence of God, so I know from experience. But I have found far more peace and happiness by accepting that God exists than I have in all my years of doubting. For the whole of human history, even the most remote tribes have acknowledged a supreme being, a creator of the world. This was their God. Faith seems more natural to me than skepticism.

I believe that hidden in a person's beliefs lay the seeds for self-fulfilling prophecies. If a person has full conviction they're going to make it to Heaven, they are going to make it there. It's like seeing it before you live it. Having this vision of the future causes one fashion their lifestyle according to their hopes. This vision becomes a goal that must be achieved. I believe the same thing happens to those who don't believe in God. If they don't believe in an afterlife or Heaven, they'll receive whatever their faith has brought them. If we envision a future bliss, we will strive for it. I would rather think the best and expect the best, than constantly insist that God and Heaven don't exist. I would rather have something to live for than nothing.

I would rather feel close to God than feel estranged.

Scientists can explain how the Earth was created, and say that God was not involved. But science cannot explain the many miracles that have happened in this world. Certain miracles of healing have baffled non-believers, and turned them into believers. Contact with mystery often inspires faith in something greater than man's limited perceptions. God provides strength and intuition. What a comforting feeling to know that my Heavenly Father loves me and wants to equip me with His strength, His Love and His Blessing. Can science provide these gifts to anybody other than a professional scientist?

YOU ARE NOT ALONE

You are not alone. The mind works in funny ways, making things sometimes appear worse than they really are. I believe the biggest thing I was lacking in my relationship with God was the feeling I was being cared for. I needed to feel a God I could not see, touch or hear, in order to believe that He loved me. I needed to know that if I loved Him, He'd love me back. It has taken me many years to understand Him, and accept the gifts He has given me. It is so very easy, yet so very hard to understand, because we as humans need to touch it, taste it, and hear it before we call it real. We need proof. But I think the strongest proof is the strength we find when we believe. Faith builds strength, strength builds faith. As I became stronger in my belief, nothing seems impossible.

Believing in God doesn't mean you're promised a bullet-proof life, full of happiness and devoid of despair. No way! There will always be circumstances that don't make sense. Bad things happen to good people. The innocent suffer. People die and murder in His name. I cannot explain why this is allowed in God's world. But if you believe in Him, you can consider this life a temporary testing ground. Our lives become a journey toward oneness with God, with death leading to the ultimate oneness. Dying means getting one step closer to God. God also plays a role in the life of people left behind. He provides understanding, and the strength necessary to make it through our times of grief and loss.

Life passes quickly. Very quickly. I can't believe how my life has flown by, how fast my kids are growing up. Time is something you can't buy. You can't stop going forward, there's no backing up. We must spend our time wisely, carefully considering what we do with it. I now must look at my life with reference to my faith. How can I spend my time in a way that honors my faith, and does justice to it? Where have critical thoughts about God gotten me these past thirty years? Nowhere. I've gained nothing but pain, a closed heart and a closed mind. I value this time on God's Earth. I will use it wisely to praise His name and build new faith. Imagine how time is experienced by God. Even our longest life-span is a tiny droplet in the ocean. But in this brief span of time we can draw near Him.

I now believe that unanswered prayers are God's way

of letting me know I'm in for a time of self-reflection. I must be tested. Will I have the strength and intuition to make the right choices? There will be times when I feel like God is right beside me, and other times I'll feel that I'm on my journey alone. But He will always be there to draw inspiration and confidence from. Life is about discovery and personal progress. We go upward in our development. God cannot always tell me the right step, but He can comfort me after I take the wrong one.

MY MUSIC TALENT IS A GIFT FROM GOD

Some of the most powerful music I've written has come from some deep place within my soul, a place I've been unable to accurately describe in the past. Sure I have given God credit for some of my songs. But looking back, I didn't give Him full credit for blessing me with inspiration, for the ability to use music as a means of self-expression. I firmly believe that this creative place inside me is a place within where God dwells.

Music has helped me to get in tune with both God and other people. I've come to know their spirits, needs and intentions. It has helped me stay grounded and real. It has allowed me to maintain a connection with my soul and spirit. I like myself and love myself, not in some self-absorbed way, not in a way that makes me egotistical or narcissistic, but in a way that allows me to be proud of how far I've come. I'm glad that in my life I have generally gone forwards instead of backwards, and that I try to improve myself in some way every single day.

I have written personally revealing songs since I was seventeen years old. The following lyrics have been put to music and professionally recorded. I have decided to share them with you so that you may see how I expressed myself during some difficult times.

I wrote "I Wanna Be A Kid" when I was thirty years old. My wife and I had been married for seven years at that point, and decided we wanted to have a child. This was a huge deal and a big step for me. Before we were married we discussed the possibility of not having children.

I was a product of a messed up relationship, and therefore had a messed up childhood. I was reluctant to bring any more children into this evil and cruel world. I now know this was the wrong attitude. When we finally decided to have a child, she was pregnant within a month. "Holy cow, that was very quick," I said. I was shocked and grew very scared wondering what kind of father I was going to be. I felt unworthy to take care of a baby angel. I was facing a flood of emotions and bad memories. I could feel the little foster kid inside me beginning to cry. I felt vulnerable. I decided to write a song to my Mom, to show her that I can be a winner and have value, and that nobody was going to stop me from soaring in my life.

This song has been an inspiration to many. This is my anthem. Its message is that if I can make it in life, then anybody can make it. I have been questioned about the meaning of the chorus, which says "Bunk to Bombay." It means a bunk bed to somewhere far away. I was tired of bunk beds at the foster homes. I just wanted to escape.

If you go to my website www.IWillNeverGiveUp.com you can hear this song and watch the music video. I am truly humbled that my song has touched so many people. I know I have made God proud by sharing this positive message.

I WANNA BE A KID
BY DEREK W.CLARK
You want to see me cry, you want to see me die,
You want to look into my eyes
And see the devil's eyes,
You want to see me smile with my battle scars
But if you look into my eyes,
You'll see an Angel's heart,
It was 1975, I was 5,

Momma I was looking at you all surprised
But you were looking at me with fear,
And all along Momma, you didn't want me here.

(Chorus)
I wanna fly, bunk to Bombay,
Here I am in this world today,
I wanna fly, bunk to Bombay
Here I am, I need a home today.
No more Foster Homes and no more Orphanage,
I just wanna be a kid.

So here I am in the struggle of the human race,
But no one wants me, my face, I feel so disgraced,
I'm just an orphan in line, like a lamb to a slaughter,
I could be a good son, but no one bothers,
Well the good Lord works in mysterious ways,
He opened Heavens gates for only one day,
And the Angels of courage and Love were sent,
There was this one loving Family, that took me in.

(Chorus)
I wanna fly, bunk to Bombay,
Here I am in this world today,
I wanna fly, bunk to Bombay
Here I am, I need a home today.

No more Foster Homes and no more Orphanage,
I just wanna be a kid.

I've got a sad past, everyday a ghost haunts me,
They can't harm me, I've got a family,
I've got a son, a wife, I've got a true life,
It's been given back to me, I'll do it right,
They'll never live the Hell that I have been through,
I can guarantee that, I swear to you,
This is real, this is my life,
If I can fly, you can fly.

(chorus)
I wanna fly, bunk to Bombay,
Here I am in this world today,
I wanna fly, bunk to Bombay
Here I am, I need a home today.
No more Foster Homes and no more Orphanage,
I just wanna be a kid.
Don't leave me alone Mom.
I just wanna be a kid.
Don't leave me alone Mom

EGO OR HUMILITY

Looking back, I see that I was a troubled soul on a spiritually self-destructive path. I had lost faith in God. I had lost faith in my ability to reach out for Him. I didn't want to deal with Him. But the main thing that was keeping me from feeling His love was very simple. A simple word to say, but not so simple to exhibit. The word is humility. My pride and ego worked against me developing the close relationship I was looking for.

Faith in God is the greatest compliment to will, determination and perseverance. For a long time, I believed I'd become successful by my own merits and sacrifice. I believed it was all me, me, and me, and that my efforts were a solo enterprise. But if I'd only had faith in a power greater than mine, I believe I would have been more unstoppable in my quest to live a successful and significant life. Faith is the secret power that can help you achieve anything you desire. Faith in yourself is one thing, but faith in God is even more powerful. Faith in yourself can lead to selfishness, cockiness, and unjustified pride. Faith in the almighty

God is completely unselfish. It removes emphasis on your ego, you become humbled, and grateful for what you have. As your faith builds in Him, the greater are your successes.

I believe God has a personal journey for each one of us. He is there to navigate for us, whispering in our ear, giving us the intuition necessary to making the choices that will lead to success.

You think you are in control of your life? Your existence? At any given moment, your life could end, just like that. No warnings, no last-minute telephone calls, no last-minute hugs or goodbyes. Nobody has control over the length of their life. Whatever control you think you have is a figment of your imagination. The truth is that we are all living on borrowed time, and must fulfill our purpose while we're here. Tomorrow is never promised. We must live today with full purpose and intention.

Our world operates on instant self-gratification. Materialism, the obsessive desire for more possessions, carries us further away from God. History shows that the most materialistic societies are also the most distant from God. With materialism, our god is the next object we covet. I have at times lived a materialistic life. I had to have the newest and coolest product, always concerned about my image. It's a rat race, a never-ending cycle. You get the new gadget, and it becomes obsolete. Then you have to get the newer gadget, in a desperate attempt to always maintain your image.

The objects that I prized inflated my ego, so that the virtue of humility became more and more obscure a concept, ever harder to believe in. I would think, "Well, I'm still pretty humble. I don't drive a Ferrari or an expensive Porsche, even though I can afford one." I was very self-contented, convincing myself that I wasn't being egotistical because I wasn't always after the most expensive car or house. But even the things that I did own distracted me from my relationship with God.

I justified going to church and tithing by telling myself it was a way for me to thank God. But I realized I was using God as an insurance policy, placating Him so that I could keep the things I already had. When I made the big money, I wanted to make more, but I never felt secure. I wanted God to help me keep what I'd earned. I wanted to stay on God's good side, just in case. I childishly believed God wouldn't allow me to lose money if I was obedient to Him. When I made business deals that were supposed to be profitable, but ended up costing me dearly, I felt like God wasn't living up to His end of the bargain—a bargain that only I had made!

This was a case of wanting more material wealth instead of wanting more spiritual wealth. What God do we follow? The God of material wealth, or the God of spiritual wealth? Money can't buy peace of mind. When you've acquired wealth, fear sets in. You become afraid of losing all that you've accumulated. Family is the most important thing above any possessions. Ego diminishes your spirit, and humility increases it. Ask yourself, do I identify myself with what I most desire? Or does what I most desire identify me? Identifying with our possessions is a poor alternative to identifying yourself by your relationship to God.

NEVER LIMIT YOUR LIFE!

I am here to tell you that abandoning God limits your life. It sets limits on your aspirations, your thinking, and your range of actions. I have a motto, Never Limit Your Life. It's now my business. You can visit www.NeverLimitYourLife.com for inspiring thoughts and information on living the unlimited life. I believe with all my heart that nothing can hold me back from achieving what I want in life. Nothing! This life is about temporary challenges, not permanent ones. There are only temporary setbacks, not permanent ones. God doesn't want us to be ordinary people. He wants us to become *exceptional* people. He doesn't want us to accept a mediocre life, a life of inaction, where we sit around wallowing in despair and apathy, thinking "Well, this the life I've been handed." God wants us to change and grow.

God wants to bless those who have the faith in Him. He doesn't want part-time believers, as I once was. He wants the believers who have faith in victory. He wants to bless us and help us fight our battles. He is there for us, but we have to first believe in Him with all of our heart.

We have to fight our way through obstacles. Maybe one of your obstacles to a relationship with God is the belief that He doesn't care about you. It is easy to give up, but life was not meant to be easy. Life is meant to challenge us, so that we can become stronger, and help others become stronger. Sometimes we like to suffer a bit longer than we needed to, even when we're aware of what we're doing. Our suffering becomes the thing we identity ourselves with. We tell ourselves we cannot excel in life because of some problem or other we can't fix. Our problems become chips on our shoulder, things we're almost proud of having. But God doesn't want us to feel validated because of our troubles, he wants us to feel validated by our overcoming them.

God can't do his part until you do your part. You have to act first. Call on Him for strength and help. Don't accept problems as a way of life. With God all things can change.

Everyone always has more in them. More stamina, more energy, more faith, more love, more charity. Give more of yourself so that your life will blossom. You are meant to break out and overcome your challenges. You have to activate your faith. You have to hold your head up high rather than hold your head down. God knows you. He knows your failures and strengths. He knows exactly what you need. He has blessed you with an unbelievable super power took kit containing your talents and strengths. These are His gifts to you. Sometimes His tools get lost because we decide to fill our tool box with other items that we think will help us better. Sometimes we believe that our tool can obtain a quick fix in a tough situation. Maybe they work for a minute but the tool will eventually break when you use it too much. We tend to collect our own tools verses God's and they eventually clutter the toolbox with the wrong tools to use in life's tough situations. I know I am guilty of thinking that my tools were better than God's. We then become hardened when we don't know the right tools to use when we are facing challenges.

God's tools are invincible and will never break. They have a lifetime guarantee. They will always be there for you through any kind of weather that you are facing. We have always been equipped with the right tools, but at times, we choose not to use them. I believe we didn't have faith in them and their ability. We generally are looking for the easier way and the quick fix to stop the suffering. We then equip ourselves with the quick fix tools and throw aside the other tools thinking that they are of no use anymore. We consider them out of style or are too old. But how long does the quick fix last? Not for eternity. We need to clean out our tool box and find the tools God has put in there and use them again.

Your life can change. Every morning is a new day. Never give up believing in yourself and your creator. It is never too late to believe again, if you should fall from faith. As long as you have breath in your lungs, you can start over. Thank God for forgiveness. He wants to forgive you and you need to forgive yourself. Get rid of the guilt for falling. Tell yourself nothing is going to stop you from realizing your destiny. Plant new seeds of belief, instead of living in the garden of doubt. There are too many weeds there. Pull the weeds up by the root and throw them out.

I AM NOT WHO I WAS

I believe that every single person on this Earth has a purpose. The purpose might be making an impact on the entire world, or it could be helping another person learn what compassion and charity are. Even the littlest things add to the overall meaning and beauty of life. Everyone has a part, whether big or small. It's a ripple effect. Positive actions have rewards for people in places you might never have anticipated.

We can not control Gods movements or purpose. He could have taken my breath of life away at any point in my existence. I have no control over my life. I only have control over my attitude towards life. Without God, we are nothing. He is the creator of real hope.

The mantra of "no pain, no gain" was my philosophy. The ability to thrive on pain was always a good ego boost. But focusing on pain, I lost the most important thing in life, and that was humility towards my past. Humility is real and ego is fake, plain and simple. God could see right through me. I hid my face in shame at times when I was yearning to know Him. It made me cold and bitter. I used egotism as a mask for the pain

I was feeling, but secretly enjoyed the chains of pain, hate and suffering that kept me bound. "Pain makes me stronger," I would say. But cherishing our pain doesn't make us stronger.

I needed God but didn't really know how to approach Him humbly. At times, my ego was meant to show God that I was good as He was. That He was not supreme to me. I made it by myself without God's help. This was wrong. I realize now that I am a care-taker of God's money and possessions. These are not mine. I do not really own them. They are made from the dirt and materials that He created. God owns the dirt. Money and possessions, in the end, are little more than an empire of dirt. When I die, none of my posses-sions can come with me. There is no U-Haul trailer on the back of my hearse, filled with all my worldly pos-sessions, so that I can furnish my home in Heaven.

Have you ever heard the saying, "I am too blessed to be stressed"? When we feel blessed, the problems we encounter in life seem inconsequential to the main thing, our relationship with God. I will never give up on God again. It is my prayer that you will be touched, and become an instrument for God. It is my prayer that you find hope in His love and strength through

His word. I hope that you will look outside and see the many beautiful miracles happening all around you, instead of all the bad things going on. I would rather walk in faith, using its power to bring about the things I believe in, than die a bitter and hardened old man who wasn't able humble himself before the Creator.

I have fallen many times, but God has helped me rise again and again. I have been broken down and made stronger. I cannot hide my weaknesses from Him. He is all-knowing. I have learned to embrace Him, even with all my faults, because I know He will continue to forgive me. If you don't feel worthy, don't worry. I have been there. You are worthy; you are His beautiful creation, His masterpiece. He made you in His image. You are meant to shine, to succeed. He is the light in your darkness. You can share this light with others in their darkness. Giving of yourself will help your soul to grow. You have the power to help others with their faith.

It all comes down to love. The way you love yourself, the way you love others, and the way you love God determines the way you look at this world. If you have love in your heart, you are free from the bitterness and negativity of this world. Just as God created you, you are the creator of your own life story.

I have a deeper appreciation for life now. There were times when I went to bed, thinking maybe, just maybe, God would deliver me from my pain. I would never have to wake up again and face the world. But something has kept me going all these years. I was just a kid looking for a reason to be alive, and didn't have a lot to be hopeful for. No longer do I cry tears of pain, but the tears of gratitude for being alive this day. As I close my eyes at night, I pray that I am able to wake up and share another day with my family. I am grateful for the breath of life I get to take in every morning. It is an amazing feeling, knowing I have another day to show God I yearn to be an instrument for Him. I will praise Him.

I thank God for the beauty of transformation. I was that old ugly caterpillar that only chomped on the weeds of pain, loneliness, and despair. The more I chomped, the more unloved I felt, the less trust I felt towards others, and the more bitter I became towards God. I finally had to spit out the bitter taste in my mouth, and take in the sweetness of God. I was chomping on the wrong plants. I could have been chomping on something more healthy for my heart, mind and spirit. But with forgiveness and the grace of God, I am transformed into a giant beautiful butterfly, soaring to new heights and new destinations, filled with simple wonder.

Just as I transformed, so can you. I know that if I can fly, you can fly. Transformation is within your grasp. Never give up!

CONTACT ME

You can contact Derek Clark at:
1-800-980-0751

Derek@iwillnevergiveup.com
Visit Derek Clark's website at
www.IWillNeverGiveUp.com
and
www.NeverLimitYourLife.com

OTHER PRODUCTS AVAILABLE FROM DEREK CLARK VISIT www.IWillNeverGiveUp.com

When Derek speaks, it is from his passionate soul. He brings along his guitar to sing the journals of his life. He believes that music is one of the purest ways to touch and communicate with the hearts of the audience. Derek Clark is an electrifying speaker whose message conveys a "realistic" mix of hope, humor, encouragement and determination. By sharing his sad and triumphant experiences, he hopes to inspire others to live their lives without limits. On stage, his passion for life and music will touch and warm the audience's soul.

To have Derek Clark be a part of your next event, please call 1-800-980-0751, or email him at seminars@IWillNeverGiveUp.com

Check out Derek Clark's Upcoming Events. The Topics Are On The Following Pages. Contact Derek Clark For More Information On How You Can Have Him Speak At Your Event.

Derek's autobiographical Book which received the highest rating of 5 Stars from the American Authors Association

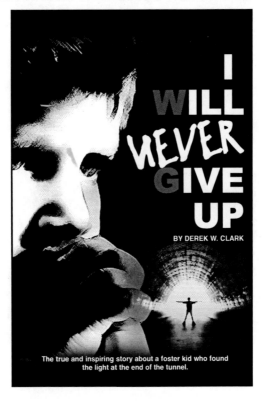